Can I tell you about Dyspraxia?

Can I tell you about...?

The "Can I tell you about...?" series offers simple introductions to a range of limiting conditions and other issues that affect our lives. Friendly characters invite readers to learn about their experiences, the challenges they face, and how they would like to be helped and supported. These books serve as excellent starting points for family and classroom discussions.

Other subjects covered in the "Can I tell you about...?" series

ADHD

Adoption

Asperger Syndrome

Asthma

Autism

Cerebral Palsy

Dementia

Diabetes (Type 1)

Dyslexia

Epilepsy

ME/Chronic Fatigue Syndrome

OCD

Parkinson's Disease

Selective Mutism

Stammering/Stuttering

Tourette Syndrome

Can I tell you about Dyspraxia?

A guide for friends, family and professionals

MAUREEN BOON

Illustrated by Imogen Hallam

Jessica Kingsley *Publishers*
London and Philadelphia

First published in 2014
by Jessica Kingsley Publishers
73 Collier Street
London N1 9BE, UK
and
400 Market Street, Suite 400
Philadelphia, PA 19106, USA

www.jkp.com

Library of Congress Cataloging in Publication Data
Boon, Maureen, 1949- author.
Can I tell you about dyspraxia? : a guide for friends,
family and professionals / Maureen Boon ;
illustrated by Imogen Hallam.
pages cm. -- (Can I tell you about--)
Audience: Ages 7+
Includes bibliographical references.
ISBN 978-1-84905-447-8 (alk. paper)
1. Apraxia--Juvenile literature. 2. Psychomotor disorders-
-Juvenile literature. I. Hallam, Imogen,
illustrator. II. Title. III. Series: Can I tell you about-- ? series.
RJ496.A63B657 2014
618.92'8552--dc23

2013048190

British Library Cataloguing in Publication Data
A CIP catalogue record for this book is available from the British Library

ISBN 978 1 84905 447 8
eISBN 978 0 85700 824 4

Printed and bound in Great Britain by Bell and Bain Ltd, Glasgow

Contents

What it's like to have dyspraxia 6

Getting dressed and changed 10

Going to secondary school 14

Before I went to secondary school 16

Early signs of dyspraxia 18

Difficulties at primary school 20

Going for an assessment 24

Therapy groups 26

Handwriting and fine motor skills 28

Getting organised for school 32

Sport 36

Maths and science 38

Some facts about dyspraxia 39

How parents can help 40

How teachers can help 42

How other children can help 46

RECOMMENDED READING, WEBSITES AND ORGANISATIONS 47

Hello. My name is Marco and I have dyspraxia.

"I'd like to tell you what it's like to have dyspraxia. Some people call it DCD, which stands for 'Developmental Coordination Disorder', especially my doctor and physiotherapists, but it means the same. People with dyspraxia are usually boys like me but there are some girls too."

"If you saw me you wouldn't know I had dyspraxia until maybe I started doing sport or something that needs good coordination, like making models or tying knots. Then you might notice that I have to work very hard to achieve what other children do without any problems. Other people sometimes think I am being lazy or careless but this isn't true.

Handwriting is also more difficult for me and I have to practise a lot and it takes me longer. Fortunately I'm great on my computer so I prefer to write on that. When teachers look at my handwriting they might at first think, because it's so untidy and difficult to read, that I am not very clever. If they ask me to read it to them they realise that I have some great ideas and usually know the answers. I find it difficult to concentrate for a long time though. When I was in the first class and I was about five years old I had to sit on a carpet with my legs crossed to listen to a story – all of us did – but for me it was a nightmare. I was so uncomfortable and used to wriggle all the time. The other children got annoyed with me bumping into them and the teacher used to tell me off."

"My friend Clara sometimes can't think
of the right word to say and clams up."

"I also tend to forget things I'm meant to take to school, like my sports kit and homework. My mum helps me with this and makes me check my bag, but it's easy for me to forget and then I get in trouble at school.

People sometimes think I'm scruffy because my clothes don't seem to look right. By the end of the day my shirt seems to have come out of my trousers, my shoes are undone and my hair is sticking up. I have to try really hard to stay tidy!

One of my friends, Clara, has a different sort of dyspraxia called verbal dyspraxia and she finds it difficult to say some sounds, like for 'more', she says 'ma'. Sometimes she just can't think of the right word to say and clams up. Clara told me that she can find reading difficult because she mixes up the sounds of the letters and words. Sometimes she doesn't understand what people say to her as they speak too quickly and she finds it very frustrating. Sometimes the other children don't understand what she says and give up trying to work it out."

"Tying laces is tricky."

"As I said before, doing fiddly things with my hands is difficult for me and that includes getting dressed for school in the morning and getting changed for sport.

When I first went to school I found it really hard to work out which shoe went on which foot. My mum colour-coded my shoes for me by putting a red mark inside the left shoe and a green mark inside the right shoe and that helped – once I remembered which foot was which colour. Also it helped me understand left and right a bit more. Laces and buckles are really tricky so Mum always buys me shoes and trainers with Velcro fittings.

At school we all have the same sort of T-shirts and shorts for PE and it's really easy to get mixed up with other people's clothes. Also as I said before, sometimes I forget things, especially as it takes me longer to get changed. When all the other children have gone and I'm running late I just stuff everything in my bag and rush off – and sometimes things fall out or get forgotten. My mum has put labels in all my clothes so I usually find them again at lost property if I'm lucky. "

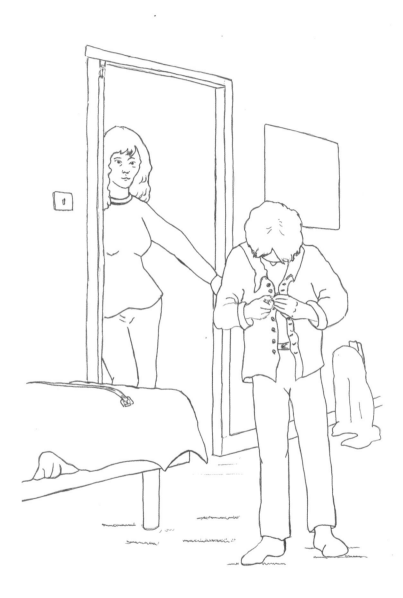

"Dressing can be very fiddly."

"Even putting on a sweatshirt can go wrong and I end up with it on the wrong way round and the logo at the back. Mum tells me to always look for the label and make sure it goes at the back. Sometimes though I do that and I end up with my sweatshirt the right way round but inside out. People think it's funny so I pretend I've done it on purpose for a joke, and then I get in trouble with the teacher again!

My school shirt has buttons down the front and I just hate doing it up after sport because I never seem to get the buttons and buttonholes in the right places! Sometimes I just pull it over my head to get undressed quickly and end up losing buttons.

I'm really glad that at my school we don't have to wear ties like my dad does. I'd never manage that. Fortunately we have ones that just stick on with Velcro.

I find I need new shoes more often than most of my friends because rather than undo them when I take them off I just pull them off, and then when I put them on again – I just push my feet in and they get trodden down on the backs. My mum is always telling me off about this.

Mum has to be careful what the clothes she buys me are made of because some clothes like sweaters can be made of wool and it makes me itch."

"They gave me a good map of the
school to find my way around."

"It wasn't so bad when I was at primary school because I knew everyone and there weren't so many teachers. It was easy to get round school because there were only four classes. When I went to secondary school it was a bit of a shock. It was so big I couldn't believe it. There were over 1,000 children there instead of less than 100 and the school was huge, it had lots of different buildings and different floors.

We went for a couple of visits when we were in the last class at primary school and my class went round together so it wasn't so bad. We were shown the room where we would go to every morning when we started in September, it was called our form room. After that we were told that we would go to different classrooms – sometimes all of the class and sometimes just some of us. They gave us a good map of the school which was colour-coded and that helped a bit."

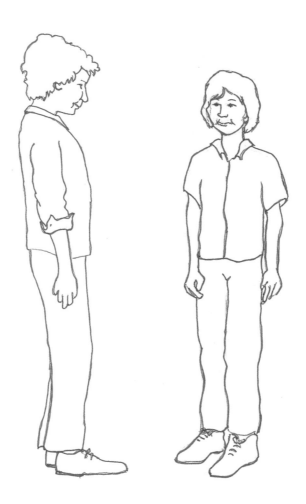

"Kevin helped me when I didn't know where to go and gave me useful tips."

"My teacher at primary school told my new school that I might have a few problems getting around and when I got there in September my new teacher introduced me to Kevin who was going to help me if I got lost. Kevin was great, he'd been at the school two years already and told me that he had the same difficulties with getting around, getting changed and losing things when he started. He explained that he would look out for me at break times and lunchtimes and check I was OK and that I knew where to go next. If I had any problems, I could talk to him and he would help sort things out.

Kevin showed me places I could go if I got lost or worried, called 'safe places' like the school nurse's room or the reception office. He showed me where the lost property office was. He said that he found things much easier now that he was used to the school.

Another thing I found tricky at secondary school was where to catch the bus to get home as there were lots of different buses.

At lunchtimes we had to use a smartcard to pay for our food (that our parents had credited with money). If you forget your smartcard you can't have anything to eat, so Mum usually puts some money in my bag just in case."

"When I was little it took me a
while to start walking."

"When I first started school Mum and Dad didn't realise I had dyspraxia. Mum told me I had been a 'bottom shuffler' when I was little, which made me laugh. They said that I didn't crawl like my twin sister Sofia but sat on my bottom and pushed myself around with my legs. I also had a little car, I sat in it and pushed myself around in it. I didn't stand up for ages but I was happy playing on the floor with my toys. Then I got a special train set for Christmas and Dad put it on a table and I had to be held up to play with it. Within a week they said I was pulling myself up and standing at the table and playing with the train. Soon after that I started walking.

Mum also said when I was little I used to hate loud noises like the vacuum cleaner. I'm OK now with that, and sometimes help out with jobs at home and can manage fine.

Another thing Dad said about me when I was a baby was that I didn't sleep well at night and kept waking my sister up. When I started walking I used to rush around and tire myself out and nap during the day, and then I wouldn't settle at night. I sleep all right now, though, and sometimes it's my sister who wakes me up, turning up her music really loud in the mornings."

"I found sitting on the carpet to listen to stories really hard."

"At school I found sitting on the carpet to listen to stories, or other things the teacher did with us, really hard. We had to sit and listen for ages and in the end I couldn't concentrate at all. I just had to move as the carpet was itchy and I couldn't sit still any longer. Sometimes I used to ask the teacher if I could go to the toilet just to stand up and move. She got a bit fed up with me as I kept asking and in the end she told me I had to wait. Even when I was sitting on the little chair at my table I sometimes fell off. We played games on the table quite a lot and I loved playing with the building blocks, but sometimes when I was concentrating on my own building I would accidentally bump the table or knock the bricks over and my buildings and the other children's buildings would fall on the floor. This sometimes made the other children fed up with me and they didn't want me to sit or play with them.

Painting was tricky too because I always found the brushes hard to use and clean and often knocked the water pot over. I used to try really hard but my pictures usually turned out messy with all the colours mixing together and the paper got so wet that it ended up with holes in it."

"I find packed lunches much
easier than school dinners."

"When we did sport at school we had to throw and catch and kick balls. I was always falling over and found it really hard to catch balls – they would just fall through my hands. Walking on benches to balance was really hard and I kept falling off. I got really fed up because the other children found everything easy. In the end I used to pretend to be sick on the days we did sport and try and stay at home. It only worked a couple of times because Mum realised what I was up to!

When we had to do writing I found it really hard to make the letter shapes for my own name. We had to use pencils and I found that my pencil kept breaking because I pressed so hard, and my letters were all over the page rather than in a straight line.

Another thing which was tricky for me was using the knives and forks at school at lunchtime. I used to find it really difficult to cut food and ended up with food all over my face and my clothes. In the end Mum used to pack me a lunch which was easy to eat, like little sandwiches and grapes – and that was much better."

"I went for an assessment and met
a physiotherapist and occupational
therapist. They were really nice."

"My teacher talked to my mum and dad and said that it might be a good idea if I saw someone called the SENCO. The SENCO is the Special Needs Coordinator and is there to help children who have any problems in school. The SENCO was called Mr Curtis and he was really kind. He got me to copy some shapes and things like that. He said he thought it might be helpful for me to see a physiotherapist (physio for short) or an occupational therapist (OT for short).

I had never heard of these people before but Mr Curtis said they would help me with sport and writing. He wrote a letter asking if I could have an assessment and Mum and Dad thought it was a good idea.

I was excited but a bit worried about the assessment but everyone was really nice. We went to a special centre and I met a physio first and she gave me all sorts of exercises to do. She had me walk on a line, climb some steps, catch balls and do some balancing. She told me I did very well and that I had worked very hard. Then I saw the occupational therapist and she asked me to write my name and copy some patterns and tried out different pencils and pencil grips to see if they helped me."

"I used to go to physio groups. It
really helped me with sport."

"The physiotherapist and OT talked to me and my mum and said that they thought it would be a good idea for me to join a group for a few weeks at the centre. I would work with other children of my age on physical activities and things like writing and cutting out with scissors. When I went along to the therapy group I was really surprised, all the other children had the same sort of problems as me and we all worked together and helped each other. I'm still friends with Dan, one of the other boys who was at the group. It's good to be able to talk to someone who has similar difficulties, as we go to different schools and we can compare what we have to do in sport and in class.

The physio group really helped me with sport at school. There were only eight of us – six boys and two girls – and we practised all the things that are hard at school. We did football skills, catching and throwing, aiming at skittles, balancing on a beam and doing exercises like forward rolls and different stretches."

"My OT helped me to improve my
handwriting by using special equipment."

"In the OT group we did a lot of work on our handwriting. The OT showed us the best position for writing and we tried out writing on sloping boards and using different pencils and grips. She gave me a sloping board and a grip which I could use at school. They were really helpful when I was at primary school but I don't need to use them now. I still angle my paper, though, as this helps too. I was also told to always use my other hand to stop the paper moving.

The OT also gave us some special lined paper to use to practise writing letters. It had straight lines and dotted lines and it was much easier to write the letters using the lines. We used little blackboards with chalk to practise writing the letters because it didn't matter how many times you tried it as you could rub it out and start again."

Marco

"This is the special paper my OT gave me.
I tried really hard and practised a lot and
managed to write my name really well!"

"We used some great scissors which you could use in your left or right hand and they cut both ways. I'm left-handed and I always had problems with the scissors in school up to then. The OT used to tell us, "Thumbs up for scissors!" We would do this and then pick up the scissors, and amazingly the scissors were in our hands the right way up!

Sometimes we practised making drinks and sandwiches. We poured juice and water into our glasses and buttered the bread with a knife. We were shown the best way to hold a knife by putting our index finger (Peter Pointer) on the top of the knife. It was really helpful because at home Mum always used to do it for me and now I can do it myself without making so much mess."

"It helps to check my bag every night."

"When you go to secondary school you have to take a lot of different things with you every day – homework, notebooks, timetable, sports clothes, books, pencils and pens, sometimes even cooking ingredients for food technology. Every day is different and it's really easy to turn up at school with the wrong things. My mum has got me in the habit of checking my school bag every evening before I go to bed. I look at my timetable and work out what I need. At first Mum used to help me but I can do it myself now. I colour-coded my timetable with Mum's help so that I could see which lessons were on which day and what I needed to take to school, for example I highlighted sport lessons as yellow and technology as green.

Being at secondary school means you have a bigger school bag which is quite heavy, and you have to take things out for different lessons and pack them back again at the end. It always takes me longer than the others and I'm always losing things like pens and exercise books."

"I use my laptop in school because it's faster for me than writing by hand."

"When I first came to the secondary school I met the SENCO here and she said it was OK to use my laptop in school because it's faster for me than writing by hand. The only trouble is that I have to carry it around with me from class to class as well as my school bag. At lunchtime I put it in my locker to keep it safe, but I have to go and get it again after lunch and sometimes I forget.

We aren't allowed to use mobile phones in school and this is a shame because I could use the phone to record what the teacher says about homework or take a photo of what's on the board. I take such a long time to write everything down at the end of a lesson that I end up late for the next class and then I find I've written in a hurry and I can't read it when I get home.

Some teachers put the homework, PowerPoint and diagrams on the school website (or intranet) and this helps a lot, but not all of them do it. I talked to the SENCO about this and she has given me special permission to use a mini iPad to record and take photos."

"I really love swimming and my
physio says it's good for me."

"My physio told me that I should do more sport. This was a surprise to me because I always tried to avoid doing sport if I could. She suggested some different types of sport such as trampolining, swimming and Tai Chi. I tried them all and they were all interesting but I really love swimming. As part of the physio group sessions we did some trampolining and Linda, our physio, called it 'rebound therapy'. It was a fantastic experience. The good thing about sports like swimming is that you are not in a team and trying to beat anyone. You are just enjoying yourself and trying to improve by swimming a bit further or a little bit faster each time.

What I don't enjoy at school are team games, especially when we have to pick teams, but fortunately my school lets you have a choice of sports activity so I usually work in the gym on the equipment, which you can do at your own level. My friend Andy has dyspraxia too and his parents found out about this when he was quite small, before he started school. He told me that his physio had recommended that he go to a gymnastics group for little children and this really helped him with doing sport when he started school because he had already learnt things like forward rolls and balancing on benches."

"I find things like mathematics difficult sometimes. It's confusing doing addition, subtraction and multiplication of big numbers because you have to line them up. If I use squared paper it makes it easier for me. Also, it's confusing because when you read and write you go from left to right but when you do maths you start on the right-hand side, except when you do long division and then you start on the left!

Since I've been at secondary school we've had to do more things with rulers, set squares and protractors. It's really hard for me to hold something like a ruler in one hand and draw a line with the other. Luckily my OT found me one which had a little knob on the top which you could hold on to and which had a sort of sticky surface so it didn't move so much.

Science is a bit scary too because we have to use Bunsen burners and I'm really scared I might knock something over. Luckily the SENCO has organised for a teaching assistant to help me and my friend Andy in the practical lessons like science and design technology. She doesn't do it for us but makes sure we're well organised and do things safely. We have really awkward stools to sit on in science which are quite high. Sometimes I just stand up to work as I don't want to fall off my stool."

Some facts about dyspraxia

- "About six children in 100 have some kind of dyspraxia.

- Another name for dyspraxia is Developmental Coordination Disorder, or DCD.

- There is no clear known cause of dyspraxia.

- People with dyspraxia find activities involving physical coordination difficult, like sport, handwriting or using scissors.

- Some people with dyspraxia find speaking and communicating difficult. This is called verbal dyspraxia.

- More boys have dyspraxia than girls. There are about four boys to every one girl.

- In a primary or elementary class of 28 children there is likely to be at least one person with dyspraxia and it will probably be a boy."

How parents can help

- "Buy shoes with Velcro fastenings – laces and buckles are really difficult for me.

- Label clothes and shoes so that when I lose them they can be found again.

- Mark shoes 'left' and 'right' inside or colour-code them so I don't get them mixed up.

- Make sure all clothes are easy to put on and that the necks are not too tight, so it's easier for me to pull things over my head.

- It's easier for me if cups are not filled up too much.

- Packed lunches are sometimes easier for me than school meals. Please make them easy to open. Yogurts are a nightmare because they splash on you when you take off the lid. Fizzy drinks seem to fizz out all over me. Crisps packets are tricky to open and I often end up with crisps all over the place. Bananas are good because they are easy to peel.

- Even though I may not like sport and exercise it's really good for me to do as much as possible. I like sport which is not competitive and where I can work on my own or alongside others, like swimming. I might try not to go into school on days when we do sport by saying that I'm sick.

- Please understand that when I am doing some things it may look as if I'm not trying, or taking too long (like dressing and writing) but I'm really working very hard and it's tiring.

- Help me organise myself by making lists and using timetables.

- Remember that some fabrics like wool may irritate me.

- I find using the computer for homework easier than writing."

How teachers can help

PRIMARY/ELEMENTARY SCHOOL

- "Remember it takes me longer to get changed than the other children and I might need some help. It's easier for me if I have a chair or bench to sit on and somewhere to put my clothes.

- Please don't make me sit on the floor for long periods as I get uncomfortable and can't concentrate. Make sure I have the right size chair to sit on. Remind me to sit properly – 'feet flat, bottom back, head in the middle', as my OT says.

- I find writing difficult especially when I start learning to write letters. Please let me use paper with wide lines and a chunky pencil. I might need a special grip on my pencil to help me. Make sure I angle my paper or book and I might need a sloping wedge to write on. I sometimes find it difficult to remember to put spaces between words and need to be reminded to use 'finger' spaces by using my finger to measure the space.

- Cutting out using scissors is really tricky to learn to do. When I was younger my OT gave me some special scissors to use.

- When we have to copy writing off the whiteboard I find it really hard to keep looking up and down. It's easier for me to copy from a print-out which is next to the book or paper I am writing on.

- I find it difficult to use small apparatus like threading beads and little bricks. Please give me something easier to hold, like bigger bricks.

- I often accidentally knock things on the floor. Please make sure I have plenty of space so I don't knock paint pots and other children's equipment off the table.

- I find all sport really difficult but it's really important that I do it as it's the only way I can improve my coordination and skills. Please make sure I have activities that I can do but don't make me work on my own with a teaching assistant as I feel left out. I like working in a group as long as I can do things OK. It can make me feel sad if I am the last to be chosen for teams so it would be great if teachers chose the teams and picked people at random.

- In maths please let me use squared paper as it's much easier to set things out. Also make sure my counters and blocks aren't really small. If I have to use a ruler it's easier if I have one which has a handle on the top and a sticky finish on the bottom so it doesn't move around. I sometimes mix up the + and × signs as they are so similar. I need to be reminded to go from right to left when I start doing long addition, subtraction and multiplication but to go from left to right for division.

- If I keep asking to go to the toilet it might be because everything has got too difficult or I need to move around for a while.

- Music is sometimes tricky for me as it's hard for me to copy rhythms and beat time. Sometimes I find it difficult to play things like drums quietly.

- Please make sure when you give the class instructions that you make each stage clear. If you say it all really quickly I get confused. I can do it but I need to know what to do at each stage.

- Make sure that all the staff I work with have copies of reports from my physio and OT so that they know how to help me. Please talk to my physio or OT and find out how they are helping me to improve.

- Remember that it takes me a great deal of effort to do what other children find easy. I really appreciate being praised for making a good effort even if I don't achieve the full task."

SECONDARY/HIGH SCHOOL

- "When I start it's really helpful to have a clear map – colour-coded if possible.

- Colour-coding helps me when I look at timetables, diagrams and written music. It also helps if they are really clear and easy to read – not too complicated.

- Having a 'buddy' to look out for me, someone who has been at the school a couple of years and understands my difficulties, is a really good idea.

- Make sure you let me know where to go if I get lost.

- I find sport really difficult but it is very good for me to improve my coordination, so please give me alternatives to team games like football and cricket.

- I might need help with equipment in science and technology as I tend to knock things over and find small apparatus difficult to use.

- Please let me use my laptop in school for writing, as for me it's much quicker than handwriting.

- Writing down notes from the board is hard for me so please give me printed handouts or let me take a photo of the board. It's really helpful if you put homework on the school website or Moodle.

- I might need extra help in exams. Please can you find out if I can have extra time, or use a computer, or have someone to write things down for me (an amanuensis)."

How other children can help

- "Don't laugh when I fall over or knock things off the table. It's an accident. Please help me tidy up the mess.

- If I forget my kit for sports lessons and you spot them in the changing room, please pick them up and bring them back to me.

- I find it difficult to remember all the things the teacher told us to do, so please help me if I ask you to tell me what the teacher said.

- Please don't ignore me in sport and when playing games. I am trying my best and working very hard. I would love someone to choose to be my partner or include me in their team.

- If I put my clothes on the wrong way round or inside out, please tell me. I might not seem very grateful but it's important that I know."

Recommended reading, websites and organisations

BOOKS FOR CHILDREN AND TEENS

Biggs, V. (2005) *Caged in Chaos: A Dyspraxic Guide to Breaking Free*. London and Philadelphia: Jessica Kingsley Publishers.

This book was written by a teenager with dyspraxia and gives a practical guide to dealing with a variety of situations.

Dixon, G. (2005) *Discover Yourself*. Hitchin: Dyspraxia Foundation.

A short book aimed at seven- to ten-year olds with dyspraxia and illustrated by children. It explains what dyspraxia is and offers positive suggestions.

Dyspraxia Foundation (2012) *My Life – Hopes and Dreams: Adventures*. Hitchin: Dyspraxia Foundation.

Non-fiction, short stories and poems by young people aged from seven to 25 years who have dyspraxia.

Edwards, N. (2004) *My Friend has Dyspraxia*. London: Chrysalis Books Group plc.

Nichol, T. (2003) *Stephen Harris in Trouble: A Dyspraxic Drama in Several Clumsy Acts*. London and Philadelphia: Jessica Kingsley Publishers.

A humorous account of life through the eyes of an eleven-year-old boy with dyspraxia.

Solihull Primary Care Trust (2004) *A Handbook for Kids who have Coordination Difficulties*.

A leaflet written by young people with coordination difficulties. A series of activity-based focus groups for children aged from eight to thirteen years was carried out and the information gathered was used to develop this booklet using the children's own words and ideas. Downloadable from Solihull Primary Care Trust: www.legacy.solihull.nhs.uk Go to 'Help and advice' page and in 'Our leaflets' box, click on 'Dyspraxia leaflet'.

BOOKS FOR PARENTS AND TEACHERS

Boon, M. (2010) *Understanding Dyspraxia*. London and Philadelphia: Jessica Kingsley Publishers.

A guide for parents and teachers including case histories.

Drew, S. and Atter, E. (2008) *Can't Play Won't Play*. London and Philadelphia: Jessica Kingsley Publishers.

Practical information, tips and hints to enable children with DCD to access and enjoy activities that other children take for granted.

Kirby, A. (1999) *Dyspraxia: The Hidden Handicap*. London: Souvenir Press.

Explains causes, symptoms and diagnostic procedures in straightforward terms. The book has chapters on parents' and the family's reactions and positive ways to cope; and on the problems faced by teenagers and adults who have dyspraxia.

Kurtz, L.A. (2007) *Understanding Motor Skills in Children with Dyspraxia, ADHD, Autism, and Other Learning Disabilities. A Guide to Improving Coordination*. London and Philadelphia: Jessica Kingsley Publishers.

This book gives practical strategies and advice for helping children with coordination difficulties.

Macintyre, C. (2009) *Dyspraxia 5–14*. Abingdon: Routledge.

Useful for teachers and parents.

Nash-Wortham, M. and Hunt, J.C. (1997) *Take Time*. Stourbridge: Robinswood Press.

Movement exercises for parents, teachers and therapists of children with difficulties in speaking, reading, writing and spelling.

Portwood, M. (1999) *Developmental Dyspraxia: Identification and Intervention. A Manual for Parents and Professionals*. 2nd edition. Abingdon: David Fulton.

A detailed description of the identification of dyspraxia and ways to support dyspraxic children.

Ripley, K., Daines, B. and Barrett, J. (1997) *Dyspraxia: A Guide for Teachers and Parents*. London: David Fulton.

A thorough guide for teachers and parents on dyspraxia, including information on assessment and how to help chidren with dyspraxia.

Sassoon, R. (2003) *Handwriting; The Way To Teach It*. London: Paul Chapman Publishing.

A useful book with a lot of practical advice on teaching handwriting for teachers.

ORGANISATIONS
UK

AbilityNet
Phone: 0800 269545 (if you call from home) or 01926 312847 (if you call from work)
Email: enquiries@abilitynet.org.uk
Website: www.abilitynet.org.uk

AbilityNet is a national charity which specialises in helping adults and children with disabilities in using computers and the Internet by adapting and adjusting technology.

ACE Education Advice & ACE Education Training
36 Nicholay Road
London
N19 3EZ
General Advice Line: 0300 0115 142
(Monday to Wednesday from 10am to 1pm. Term time only)
Website: www.ace-ed.org.uk

ACE is an independent national education advice centre which offers confidential advice to parents. It also publishes a number of guides and handbooks relating to various areas of education.

AFASIC
First Floor, 20 Bowling Green Lane
London
EC1R 0BD
Helpline: 0845 355 5577 (Monday to Friday, 10.30am to 2.30pm)
Website: www.afasic.org.uk

AFASIC represents children and young adults with communication impairments. The organisation provides support for parents, carers and professionals working with these children through conferences, activity weeks, summer schools, regular newsletters and local support groups.

Contact a Family
209–211 City Road
London
EC1V 1JN
Phone: 020 7608 8700
Helpline: 0808 808 3555
Textphone: 0808 808 3556 (Freephone for parents and families: Monday to Friday, 10am to 4pm; Monday also 5.30 to 7.30pm)
Email: info@cafamily.org.uk
Website: www.cafamily.org.uk

Contact a Family aims to encourage mutual support between families whose children have disabilities and special needs by linking them through support groups and newsletters.

Dyscovery Centre
Allt-yr-yn Campus, 12 Cathedral Road
Newport
NP20 5DA
Phone: 01633 432330
Email: dyscoverycentre@newport.ac.uk
Website: http://dyscovery.newport.ac.uk/dyscovery/index.aspx

The centre offers assessment, treatment and teaching for children, adolescents and adults with dyspraxia and dyslexia.

Dyspraxia Foundation
8 West Alley
Hitchin
Herts
SG5 1EG
Phone: 01462 455016 (administration)
Helpline: 01462 454986 (Monday to Friday, 10am to 12 noon)
Email: dyspraxia@dyspraxiafoundation.org.uk
Website: www.dyspraxiafoundation.org.uk

The Dyspraxia Foundation aims to promote the awareness and understanding of dyspraxia and to support individuals and families affected by it. The organisation has local groups across the UK and publishes a regular newsletter.

National Association of Special Educational Needs
4–5 Amber Business Village
Amber Close
Amington
Tamworth
B77 4RP
Phone: 01827 311500
Email: welcome@nasen.org.uk
Website: www.nasen.org.uk

The aims of NASEN are to promote the interests of those with exceptional learning needs and/or disabilities; to provide a forum for those actively involved with exceptional learning needs and/or disabilities; and to contribute to the formulation and development of policy. NASEN publishes two journals and a magazine/newsletter.

National Parent Partnership Network
8 Wakley Street
London
EC1V 7QE
Phone: 020 7843 6058
Email: nppn@ncb.org.uk
Website: www.parentpartnership.org.uk

National Parent Partnership Network gives support to parents
and carers of children and young people with special educational
needs. They provide confidential and impartial advice.

Tai Chi News
Email: info@meiquan.co.uk
Website: www.taichinews.com/classes/children

The newsletter of the Mei Quan Academy of Tai Chi. Information
about Tai Chi and classes in the London area.

Tumble Tots, Gymbabes and Gymbobs
Tumble Tots (UK) Limited
Blue Bird Park
Bromsgrove Road
Hunnington
Halesowen
West Midlands
B62 0TT
Phone: 0121 585 7003
Website: www. tumbletots.com

The website gives contact information for local groups.

UK Tai Chi
Park View
Potterton Park
Potterton
Barwick-in-Elmet
Leeds
LS15 4NN
Phone: 07771 850129, 07765 406995, 0113 393 5005
(Monday to Friday, 9am to 6pm)

Website: www.uktaichi.com/children.html

Information and training courses for schools.

Youth Sport Trust
Sport Park
3 Oakwood Drive
Loughborough
Leicestershire
LE11 3QF
Phone: 01509 226600
Email: info@youthsporttrust.org
Website: www.youthsporttrust.org

The Youth Sport Trust supports a number of initiatives for a range of age groups: Active Play for four- to seven-year-olds; Start to Play for children under five.

Republic of Ireland

Dyspraxia Association of Ireland
Carmichael House
North Brunswick Street
Dublin 7
Phone: 01 8747085
Email: info@dyspraxia.ie
Website: www.dyspraxia.ie

Promoting awareness of dyspraxia in Ireland in order to create a better understanding of the difficulties children and parents face.

USA

Dyspraxia Foundation USA
910 West Huron Street, Unit 302
Chicago, IL 60642
Phone: (312) 489 8628 (Monday to Friday, 9am to 5pm)
Website: www.dyspraxiausa.org

Information and resources for those with dyspraxia and their families.

My Gym
Website: www.my-gym.com

Find out where the nearest My Gym club is. Different programmes are offered for children from six weeks to 13 years of age.

Tai Chi for Kids
Phone: (970) 925 1130
Email: taichiforkids@gmail.com
Website: www.taichiforkids.com

Information on Tai Chi programmes for children, including instructional videos and workshops.

Canada

AQED (Association Québécoise pour les Enfants Dyspraxiques)
C.P 26024, Fleurimont
Sherbrooke
Quebec
J1G 4J9
Phone: (819) 829 0594
Email: dyspraxieaqed@hotmail.com
Website: www.dyspraxie-aqed.ca

The association aims to give information about dyspraxia and support parents of children with dyspraxia.

Australia

Australian Dyspraxia Support Group & Resource Centre Inc.
PO Box 5519
South Windsor
NSW 2756
Phone: +61 2 45870214
Email: information@dyspraxia.com.au
Website: www. dyspraxia.com.au

The Australian Dyspraxia Support Group & Resource Centre raises awareness and understanding of dyspraxia. They provide a telephone helpline, support and resources.

New Zealand

Dyspraxia Support Group of New Zealand Inc
PO Box 20292
Bishopdale
Christchurch
Phone: 03 358 3249
Email: dyspraxia.centre@xtra.co.nz
Website: www. dyspraxia.org.nz

A support group to empower all people experiencing the impact of developmental dyspraxia. It aims to increase knowledge and understanding of developmental dyspraxia and to ensure that children/families impacted by developmental dyspraxia are supported with the resources and opportunities to reach their full potential.

Blank, for your notes